This book belongs to:

_____

Samson

Benny

Larry

Ryan

Bridget

Nigel

STARRING

This is a Parragon book
First published in 2006

Parragon
Queen Street House
4 Queen Street
Bath, BA1 1HE, UK

ISBN 1-40546-611-1
Printed in Italy

Disney's
THE WILD

p

It had been a bad day for Ryan, the young lion. It all started to go wrong when his latest attempt to roar had resulted in nothing but a pathetic squeak. Ryan had never heard the zoo visitors laugh so loudly. Then his dad, Samson the Wild, had made him look even more of a fool by letting out a terrific, crowd-pleasing roar! It was the kind of roar that only a lion that had once lived in the Wild could do.

Ryan was thoroughly sick of being himself. And now his father had the nerve to ask him why he spent so much time sulking in his tree.

"You know what I'm doing in my tree?" Ryan yelled. "I'm thinking how great it would be if Samson the Wild wasn't my father. Because it would make being Ryan the Lame a whole lot easier."

The day got even worse when Ryan accidentally made the gazelles stampede through the turtle-curling championship, causing Samson's team to lose the match. Samson watched in despair as Ryan ran off into the night.

Samson just didn't know what to do about Ryan.

"You have to tell him the truth," insisted Benny
the squirrel. Benny was Samson's best friend.

"I don't think I can do that," replied Samson. "I mean,
what will he think of me?" He didn't want to tell Ryan that
he was not really from the Wild.

Samson went off in search of Ryan. He wondered if he
would ever have the courage to tell his son that his stories
of bravery out in the Wild were just that – *stories*.

Meanwhile, Ryan had just
spotted the green boxes on the
other side of the fence. They were the crates
that went to the Wild. This was his chance
to experience the Wild and find his roar.
When no one was looking, Ryan
climbed over the fence
and hid inside one
of the crates.

Shortly afterwards, the crate was loaded on to a truck. Suddenly, Ryan changed his mind.

"Wait! I don't want to go! HELP ME!" Ryan shouted at the top of his voice.

He shouted so loudly that Samson heard him and raced towards the fence to see what was happening.

"Daaaaad!" screamed Ryan.

But even Samson's powerful claws couldn't break through the metal fence.

Soon Ryan and the truck were out of sight. Samson desperately needed to know where they were going.

Benny and Samson went to ask the pigeons for help. One of them, Hamir, told them that the green boxes went to the big water near the lady with the points on her head (which was pigeon talk for the harbour near the Statue of Liberty). He said the boxes left there at sunrise never to return.

Back at the zoo fence, Samson's friends were waiting.
Bridget the giraffe, Larry the anaconda and Nigel the koala
were all rallying round wanting to help. But it was soon
decided that Samson and Benny would embark on a rescue
mission. The others would stay behind.

Samson and Benny hid in a skip. The following morning the skip was emptied into a dustbin lorry bound for the city.

"Don't worry about a thing, big guy," said Benny. "I know this city like the back of my paw…"

But before he had time to finish, Bridget emerged from the rubbish, knocking the little squirrel off the lorry. Larry's head popped up beside Bridget. Then Samson found Nigel buried among the sacks.

It was only then that they realized Benny was missing…

When the rubbish truck stopped, the rescue party only just managed to escape without being crushed in its jaws. They were just recovering their breath, when they were surrounded by three snarling dogs.

"Run!" screamed Samson.

The gang eventually managed to escape the dogs by dropping down into the sewer.

"Why didn't you lionise those dogs?" Bridget asked.

"I don't have time to fight dogs," explained Samson. "I have to find Ryan."

Soon the gang bumped into
a pair of alligators, called Stan
and Carmine. They were proud
New Yorkers and happily gave
Samson and the others directions
to the harbour loading dock.

The gang arrived just in time to see
the ship containing Ryan's crate chugging out to sea.

Suddenly, the dock the animals were standing on began
to move. They were actually standing on a ship – a ship being
steered by a man. They had to get rid of him. Bridget stood
on Samson's tail. Samson gave a terrible roar and the terrified
captain jumped overboard, leaving Samson to take the wheel.

It wasn't too long before Samson got the hang of the steering. Then suddenly, out of nowhere, Benny appeared on the back of a goose. They crash-landed on the boat, along with the rest of the flock.

As luck would have it, the geese were seasoned travellers and they assured Samson that they would be able to keep track of Ryan's ship.

Samson followed the geese day after day, until finally both their ship and Ryan's reached a volcanic, African island.

Crates were being thrown from Ryan's ship down to where animals were waiting to be loaded. It looked like some sort of animal rescue.

Ryan's crate was thrown from the ship and cracked open. The young lion bolted for freedom, with Samson in hot pursuit. He thought he had Ryan's scent but it turned out to be a hyrax. When Samson refusd to eat the hyrax his friends were disappointed. They expected more from Samson the Wild!

The time had arrived for Samson to come clean. He explained to his friends that he was a fraud and a liar. He'd never been to the Wild before in his life. Then he turned and fled into the jungle.

The others headed back to the boat, feeling vulnerable and afraid. Benny had just convinced them to stay and find Ryan, when Nigel suddenly disappeared. Moments later the other three were surrounded by a herd of crazed-looking wildebeests.

"Don't worry. They're vegetarians," said Benny nervously.
"Then why are they licking their chops?" wailed Bridget.
A particularly mean-looking wildebeest, called Blag,
charged at Bridget. As Benny tried to defend her, he was
rammed against a rock and knocked out. Bridget and Larry
were captured and led away.

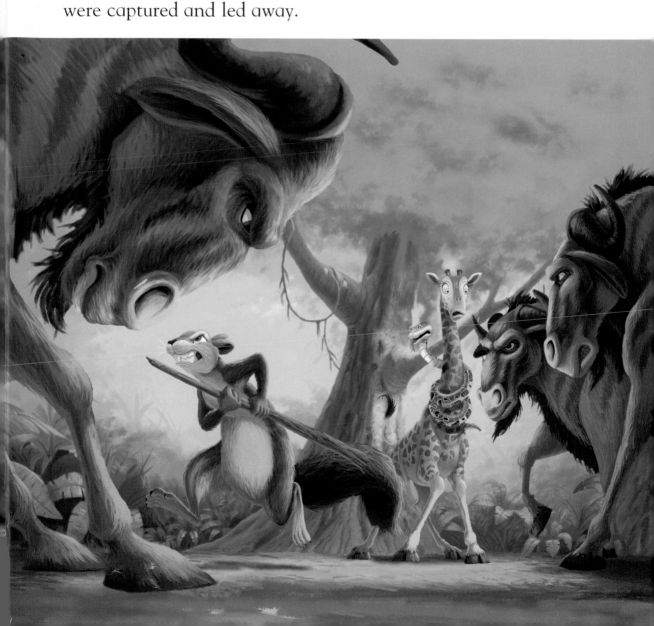

Meanwhile, the beasts had taken Nigel to a cave under the volcano where some sort of weird ceremony was taking place. Nigel was placed on a throne and presented to their leader, Kazar.

The entire wildebeest nation bowed before Nigel. Kazar pointed to a toy koala sitting on a pedestal. It was the same sort of toy koala that was sold in the zoo's giftshop.

Kazar explained that long ago the toy had fallen from a plane and startled a pack of lions that were about to pounce on him. Now the crazy wildebeests were convinced that Nigel was a god! A god who had come to lead them to the top of the food chain where they would be the hunters, not the hunted.

In another part of the island two vultures who worked for Kazar had spotted Ryan roaming through the jungle. The vultures flew back to the volcano to tell him they had found a lion.

"Did you come across his father?" asked Nigel.

"You've brought two lions?" asked Kazar. He couldn't believe Nigel's generosity.

Kazar ordered a group of wildebeests to go with the vultures to fetch the lions.

The wildebeests stamped their hooves in praise of Nigel. The koala began to think that being a god wasn't so bad, after all.

When the vultures found
Ryan they dive-bombed him.

"Help!" screamed Ryan.

Samson heard him scream and raced to the rescue.
When the vultures saw the huge lion they made a quick
escape. But before Ryan and Samson had a chance to speak,
the wildebeests turned up.

"Run!" shouted Samson, and the pair zigzagged their way
through the jungle, until they found a tree to hide in.

Ryan was puzzled. He couldn't understand why his father
wasn't fighting off the attackers.

Quickly, Samson explained that he wasn't who Ryan thought he was. He wasn't from the Wild. He was a reject from the circus. On his command performance, he had let out a tiny squeal instead of a roar and his father had disowned him. After that, Samson had been shipped to the zoo.

Suddenly, the wildebeests rammed the tree. Ryan fell and was captured, but Samson was hurled over the edge of a cliff. Ryan saw his father hit the ground far below.

The wildebeests took Ryan to the volcano, where he was reunited with Larry and Bridget.

When Blag explained what had happened to Samson, Kazar was furious. With only one small lion, there would only be enough meat for HIM to ascend to the top of the food chain.

Back out in the jungle, Benny had woken up and found Samson. The lion was weak and dazed from his fall, but determined to rescue his son and his friends.

As they set off through the dense foliage, they met a group of chameleons. They were secret agents on a mission to stop the wildebeests' evil plan. Their leaders, Cloak and Camo, were masters of camouflage. Cloak agreed to show Samson and Benny where Ryan was being held.

Inside the volcano, Larry, Bridget and Ryan were being presented to 'The Great Him' who, to their surprise, turned out to be Nigel!

Kazar was determined to cook all three of his prisoners and Nigel was doing his best to stall for time. Suddenly, Nigel rose into the air and spun in circles. Samson – cloaked in the invisible camouflage of his chameleon comrades – had lifted him up to create a diversion.

While Kazar and the others were distracted, Benny led Bridget, Larry and Ryan away to safety.

Suddenly, the cavern began to shake.

"Volcanic gas!" warned Cloak.

The chameleons that were cloaking Samson scurried away in fear, leaving Samson in full sight of the wildebeests. Kazar really thought his luck had turned.

When Ryan saw that his dad was alive, he rushed to his side.

"We can kick their rumps!" insisted Ryan. "It'll be just like in your stories."

Suddenly, the wildebeests surrounded Samson. Kazar charged and a mighty battle ensued. Unfortunately, Samson was definitely coming off worse.

Ryan had an idea. He got Larry to create a giant catapult by lashing himself between two stalagmites. Then Ryan got his friends to fire him towards the fight.

Ryan let out a deep, menacing, totally WILD roar as he landed on Kazar. But Kazar threw him to the ground.

"Finish them!" Kazar ordered the wildebeests.

To Kazar's surprise, the wildebeests didn't move. They were sick and tired of the evil Kazar and his orders.

"Get away from my son!" bellowed Samson. He pounced on Kazar with a fierce, primal ROAR that threw the wildebeest across the cavern. The roar was so loud that the earth began to shake. The volcano was about to blow!

Samson quickly led everyone to safety. They all piled on board the boat, including the herd of reformed wildebeests.

As they sailed away, the volcano spewed out a tiny black object – it was the toy koala. It landed at Nigel's feet, but much to everyone's relief he tossed it overboard.

Samson and Ryan shared a hug.

"At least I saw the Wild before it disappeared," said Ryan.

"I can still see it, it's right...."

"Here," said Ryan, interrupting his dad. He was pointing to his heart.